Milan Church Ayres

Phillips Brooks in Boston

Five years' editorial estimates

Milan Church Ayres

Phillips Brooks in Boston
Five years' editorial estimates

ISBN/EAN: 9783337141639

Printed in Europe, USA, Canada, Australia, Japan

Cover: Foto ©Andreas Hilbeck / pixelio.de

More available books at **www.hansebooks.com**

PHILLIPS BROOKS IN BOSTON

FIVE YEARS' EDITORIAL ESTIMATES

BY

M. C. AYRES

Editor of the Boston " Daily Advertiser "

With an Introduction

By Rev. W. J. TUCKER, D.D.

*Professor of Sacred Rhetoric and the Pastoral Charge in Andover
Theological Seminary, and President-elect of
Dartmouth College*

BOSTON
GEORGE H. ELLIS, 141 FRANKLIN STREET
1893

GEO. H. ELLIS, PRINTER, 141 FRANKLIN ST., BOSTON.

To Newspaper Men and Women

𝕴 Dedicate

This Memorial of one who was our Friend, as we were his.

M. C. A.

CONTENTS.

CONTENTS

4

PREFACE.

In the Prayer-Book there is a form of supplication "for all sorts and conditions of men." The editor of a daily newspaper, to be fit for his work, must constantly study, not necessarily the wishes, but the wants of those included within the entire scope of that comprehensive prayer. It was my deep certainty that Phillips Brooks was the one man in this day and generation who could best meet the religious needs of all sorts and conditions of men which led me to undertake, five years ago, the task of pointing out to the miscellaneous public, through the editorial columns of the *Advertiser*, certain characteristics of Boston's greatest preacher, and to pursue this plan systematically from year to year. There were reasons why it seemed that in some respects a "secular" journal would be a better medium than any other.

There are five conditions or tendencies which mark the attitude of large classes of people toward the Christian Church at the present time. First, there is profound discontent with regard to the lack of church unity. Second, there is a vast though as yet largely vague movement along lines of new theological thinking. Third, the thing that, for want of a better term, is called agnosticism, has a powerful hold upon many educated minds and upon many more minds that wish to be thought educated. Fourth, a still more deadly danger to religion comes from a condition which is neither hostility nor uncertainty, but simply indifference. Fifth, the intellectual and material tendencies of the time are so smothering men's spiritual nature that the word "goodness," whether in its religious or moral meaning,—though in very truth this is a distinction without a difference,—has come to signify, to multitudes of understandings, something which outwardly is "damned with faint praise," while inwardly it is despised.

With respect to each and all of these current facts, I thought it worth while to put forth even such humble and feeble efforts as I could with a view to bringing yet more widely to bear the influence of Phillips Brooks in teaching clergymen how to preach and laymen how to listen. The hope that Christian unity is to be obtained by inducing all the separate sects to come over and join some one sect is chimerical to the last degree, and growing more evidently so every day. But "the unity of the spirit in the bond of peace" is more nearly possible to-day than it has been before for a thousand years. When that is perfected, a mighty stride will have been taken toward the answer to the prayer of Jesus, "That they all may be one." I heard the rector of Trinity Church say, once, that birds, flying through the air, are not troubled how to cross our rivers. It was by lifting our conception of what the Church really is into a region far above denominational boundaries that he showed us how little need there is for such separations.

He was in profound sympathy with what is called the new theology; but he attached far more importance to its spirit than to its letter. It meant with him, not so much a new set of doctrines as a new, a broader, freer, and more spiritual use of all doctrine, so that the most conservative and the most progressive believers found their souls fed in listening to him. Though he never preached for the sake of winning theological converts, many prejudices against advanced opinions were removed by the discovery that the religious uses for which outworn dogmas are valued can be found in connection with the fresher, more rational thought of the modern era. He taught the Church how to hold on to the past, while gladly welcoming the present and the future.

He disarmed scepticism by presenting religious faith in its simplicity, sufficiency, and sublimity. He did not demand less belief than man had before been called upon to grant, but more; yet the old antagonism between reason and revelation disappeared, because he made men see that the essence of revelation is in the outreach of the divine mind to the human. Dr. Brooks overcame indifference to religious concerns by two methods. He entered into all sorts and conditions of human life with such subtle insight and imaginative sympathy that people realized for the first time that religion had something to give which they had been craving without knowing what or why; and he revealed to this humdrum, workaday world of ours the glory of the commonplace. What Macaulay said of Lord Bacon could be said, with a slight verbal change, of Bishop Brooks. He preached about things in which

everybody was interested, in language which everybody
understood.

It is requisite, but it is not easy, to touch upon that quality in him which was, after all, the most precious, peculiar,
and wonderful. It is not easy, because the theme seems
almost too sacred for words. That which most impressed
the people whose privilege it was to know him nearly—
and that inestimable privilege was freely bestowed upon
the high and lowly, rich and poor, learned and unlearned,
old and young, religious and irreligious—was not his
greatness, though no one could escape the sense of the
man's tremendous intellectual power. It was not his extraordinary eloquence. It was not his fine culture, his
varied knowledge, his indescribable keenness and brilliancy, or the charm and magnetism of his personal presence. The thing that seemed supreme in Phillips Brooks
was his goodness. I have said that the word "goodness"
has come to be despised. Who can deny that this is so?
We hear it used as the antithesis of greatness. We hear
it pronounced with a circumflex inflection. The idea pre-
vails that goodness is admirable in children, quite appropriate in women, characteristic of childlike and feminine
men, but out of place in men of the world. The fault
is partly chargeable to certain tendencies of the age in
which we live, but more to the false definition that good
people, by precept and example, have given the word.
Bishop Brooks did this crowning service, that he made
goodness mean the grandest thing of which humanity can
conceive. His was no such goodness as we attach in
thought to those whose names figure in the saints' calen-

dar. It was as far removed from the cloister as the east from the west. It was virile. It was instinct with life. It was wholesome. It was such as seemed every way suited to the pew as well as the pulpit, to the counting-house, the shop, and the drawing-room, State Street, the Back Bay, the North End. It won the hearts of students at Harvard University and of day-laborers who thronged to hear him in Faneuil Hall.

I am writing on the day when the Church commemo-rates the resurrection of her crucified Lord. This is the first of these anniversaries to occur since that voice which never seemed so eloquent as at Easter-tide was hushed in the silence of death. Not until now have we so realized our unspeakable loss. And, when we try to find language in which to clothe our remembrance of the Bishop's char-acter, all descriptions fall short, save one. I do but re-peat what, in all reverence and thoughtfulness of the words' import, many have said already, when I add my poor tribute of testimony that, far beyond all other men whom we have known in life or through extant human records, the goodness of Phillips Brooks helps toward an understanding of what that of Jesus, the Christ, must have appeared to be to those who lived in Jerusalem in the first century, as we live in Boston in the nineteenth century.

MILAN CHURCH AYRES.

BOSTON, Easter, 1893.

INTRODUCTION.

The career of Phillips Brooks, although singularly unmarked by those incidents which are supposed to attract the attention of the daily press, was yet a frequent subject of editorial comment. I know of no man of like prominence, of whom there was so little to be reported, concerning whom it was necessary to say so much. The personal reminiscences which have been printed since his death would hardly suggest to a stranger the flavor of his personality. His sermons and addresses owed nothing in the way of popular impression to " occasions " or " subjects." It was not necessary to follow his utterances upon the controversies or even the reforms of the day. He was not by first intention a reformer : he was in no sense a controversialist. Until the question of his election to the

bishopric arose, there was nothing except himself to hold him so steadily and vividly before
the public eye.

And yet no man ever held by any force of
circumstance so secure a position in the public
thought and affection as he held by the quality
of his personality. His personality made him
a vital part of his and our generation. He was
inseparable from all that is best in it, its courage,
sympathy, faith, and unquenchable hope. One
could not think of that best thing in our common Christianity, its spirit,— which we all agree
in wanting, however much we may disagree about
the way of getting it,— without thinking of him
as its representative. He was a great Christian,
reviving the ancient splendor of the Christian
name, and illustrating the perfect adaptability of
the Christian ideal to the nineteenth century.
By common consent no one has translated so
much of the Christian religion into current
thought and life as Phillips Brooks.

The secular press was quick to recognize

and acknowledge in Mr. Brooks the presence
of a religious genius. And its judgment re-
flected as much honor upon itself as upon him.
Its appreciation of him was no criticism of the
Church or of the current Christianity, but rather
a free and willing tribute of that which was
truest and finest in the religious spirit and
hope and purpose of the time. Hence the interest which was taken in the succession of the
bishopric made vacant by the death of Bishop
Paddock. Apart from the possibility of the
election of Mr. Brooks, the question would have
had only the ordinary ecclesiastical significance.
But with that possibility it was instinctively
felt that the opportunity had come to do a
supreme act in the furtherance of Christianity.
There was never any reason to doubt the sin-
cerity, any more than the insight, of the secular
press in its advocacy of the election of Mr.
Brooks to the Episcopal see of Massachusetts.

The editorial utterances of the Boston *Daily
Advertiser*, which have been gathered up in this

volume, cover only the last five years; but they
antedate by a considerable time the official life
of Bishop Brooks. And the editorials which
precede his election show the same understanding of the man, the same appreciation of his
power, the same acknowledgment of his representative character, as those which follow.
The consistency of the thought running through
these pages is everywhere manifest. The same
tone is maintained throughout. There is no
exaggeration as the discussion in regard to the
bishopric grows earnest and intense, nor yet as
the voice of congratulation is changed so sud-
denly into that of lamentation. The editorial
upon "The Great Grief," though vibrating with
the passionate sympathy of the hour, is written
with as true and steady a hand as that which
penned the study of the source of "Phillips
Brooks' Power." The death of Bishop Brooks
called forth the appropriate estimate of his marvellous influence, but the estimate was no after-
thought.

It is in every way fitting that these papers
should be brought together and given permanent form. They were written under the influence of personal gratitude and affection. When
the writer was a student at New Haven, the
lectures of Mr. Brooks were the great formative
influence in his personal and professional life.
The same influence continued as the writer was
led to Boston, and was brought into more permanent relation with the work and teachings of
Mr. Brooks. The sentiments therefore which
found expression from time to time in the editorial pages of the *Advertiser*, whether in the
form of studies, or discussion, or tribute, were to
an unusual degree personal in their character
and motive.

But, quite apart from their origin, these articles
have a permanent representative value. They
show precisely what men thought of Phillips
Brooks before the process of idealization began.
Here was one who was not greatly misunder-
stood or unappreciated in his own time. Here

was a prophet "acceptable in his own country."
Here was a representative of Christianity of
whom his fellow-Christians said with one accord,
even in a period marked by no little of contro-
versy and variance, "This man belongs to us
all : he is an assurance and sign of the coming
unity." And men at large felt that he was more
human because more Christian, that he was in
some very real sense, in his own person, a type
of the larger humanity.

The future historian will turn to such contem-
porary papers as these for the material on which
to base his estimate of the social and spiritual
life of this generation. Meanwhile those who
knew Phillips Brooks will find in these particular
papers some of the most discriminating and
appreciative of all the judgments passed upon
him, interwoven with those events in his later
public life which naturally called them forth.

WILLIAM JEWETT TUCKER.

ANDOVER, MASS., April 24, 1893.

PHILLIPS BROOKS IN BOSTON.

A MORE EXCELLENT WAY.

[March 26, 1888.]

In the course of his " Lyman Beecher Lectures on Preaching," delivered before the divinity students of Yale College in the winter of 1876-77, the Rev. Phillips Brooks, D.D., took occasion to comment on the short and easy explanations which are frequently offered to account for the phenomenal success of a particular clergyman. Sometimes the secret is thought to lie in his elocution, sometimes in his personal presence, sometimes in his choice of simple, or, again, of ornate diction. The lecturer told of an instance where he had heard the power of a pulpit-orator of great renown ascribed to the sweetly impressive manner in which he raised his hand ! Against all such shallow judgments Dr. Brooks protested, declaring that any true success, in the pulpit as out of the pulpit, must be a complex result, issuing from many and deep springs of power.

Of all that the eloquent rector of Trinity said on this subject he himself supplies an illustration. Everybody recognizes his wonderful success in winning earnest attention to religious teachings; but there are many different ways of accounting for it. On a few points, indeed, all critics agree. That Phillips Brooks is eloquent, impassioned, imaginative, analytical, liberal, a man of virile intellect and, withal, most devout faith, is apparent to every listener. But this does not suffice to solve the problem. Each of these qualities is to be found in other clergymen. And, if their combination in a single individual is rare, still the fact remains that the difference in results is out of all proportion to the difference in the qualities which are obvious to every observer. What is that additional something which we must find in our great preacher if we are at all to understand why he towers above his brethren, as much in achievement as in stature?

In attempting to answer this question, we are driven once more to the preacher's own words as the best illustration of his own characteristics. At the close of the series of lectures at New

Haven already referred to, an hour was set aside by Dr. Brooks for hearing and answering any questions which the students might put to him. One of the questions was, "What do you think of Dwight L. Moody?" And the instantaneous answer was, "What impresses me most about Mr. Moody is the astonishing good sense of the man." While all men would heartily assent to the statement that Phillips Brooks has abundantly the quality alluded to, it is probable that few, if any, of his admirers have thought of enumerating that among the secrets of his eminence. Good sense seems like such a plain and homely thing that we are accustomed to speak of it as "common sense." Probably the reason why the rector of Trinity is so quick to discern, and so delighted to discern, good sense in other men is that, in some subtile way, he feels how dominant it is over his own career. Let one look closely into the methods of Trinity pulpit, and he will find that what is said and done there is made up of certain commanding qualities, such as we have noticed above, such as it is impossible not to recognize, plus good sense. Only it is not exactly "common sense," or, if we call it that, we must needs have recourse to the threadbare say-

ing that "'common sense' is very uncommon."
It is exceedingly good sense, delicate and con-
summate good sense, good sense which rises to
a height level with genius.

A few instances must suffice. The church is
crowded by people eager only to hear the sermon. Does the preacher slight the service, that
the sermon may stand out in brighter contrast?
A popular preacher who lacked something of the
highest title to popularity would do that. Not so
this man. He puts into his utterance of creed
and litany and prescribed forms of prayer such
wealth of personal consecration that a person
who should hear that, and nothing more, would
remember the thrilling experience all his days.
Dr. Brooks is known as a "Broad Churchman,"
but he preaches neither to defend the Broad
Church nor to attack the High Church. He
shares the spirit of the "new theology"; but
probably no man ever heard him try to prove the
new or to disprove the old. Yet certainly no
man ever listened to him without discovering
that the preacher's theological attitude is open as
the sunlight.

This is the lesson which Trinity pulpit has for
every earnest preacher of every denomination.

Do not attempt to imitate Phillips Brooks in those gifts with which nature endows each man as she will, and of which Boston's beloved clergyman has received so much more than most mortals, but learn from the example set in that pulpit how to do the work which is given you to do in " a more excellent way."

DR. BROOKS' LENTEN LECTURES.

[March 29, 1888.]

While Rev. Morgan Dix, D.D., rector of Trinity Church in New York, has been startling the religious and secular world by his Lenten lectures against what he considers the sins of modern life, especially in relation to society, literature, and art, the still more eminent rector of Trinity Church in Boston, Rev. Phillips Brooks, D.D., has devoted himself to the task of expository discourse. In doing this throughout the Lenten season now drawing to a close, Dr. Brooks has followed a custom of his own from which he has not deviated for a number of years. Whatever may be the merits or demerits of the method pursued by Dr. Dix, this year as formerly, our purpose at present is not to discuss that somewhat vexed question, but rather to study briefly the lessons afforded by the widely contrasted practice of Boston's famous divine.

Nothing could ordinarily be more unpromising than a series of expository sermons or lectures.

But the genius of Phillips Brooks is shown, in this connection as in so many others, by his ability to glorify the commonplace. His expository method is as follows : He considers his subject in general and in particular. But the comprehensive statements deal only and instantly with the very vital essence of the matter, setting out in two or three bold strokes a picture of the scene or the occasion, declaring with incisive precision the purpose which was uppermost in the writer's mind. And the details are taken, not seriatim, but for their fitness to elucidate the subject. Two men with pallet and brush sit down before a landscape. One attempts to paint everything, each tree, each leaf on the tree, rocks and pebbles and sand, every separate blade of grass. The other artist delineates those features of the scene which give definiteness to the entire picture. Space, perspective, light and shade, earth and sky, are indicated ; and for detail there is such and so much as will suggest the truth and beauty of the whole. The former method is that of ordinary expository preachers. The latter method is that of Phillips Brooks.

We can best make our meaning plain by reference to some of the Lenten lectures delivered in

Trinity Church in this city during the past four seasons. In 1885 there were half a dozen lectures on the Pauline Epistles. In 1886 the chief series of lectures dealt with "certain great chapters in the greatest of the Gospels,"—the Gospel according to John. One year ago Dr. Brooks discussed "The Conversations of Jesus." This year an entirely new field was entered upon by taking up and considering various parts of the Book of Common Prayer. In discussing the writings of the Apostle Paul, Dr. Brooks brought forward in a most vivid way the personal element in the writer, and in those whom the writer was addressing. The mighty place which belongs to human affections in every institution or movement affecting for good the destinies of mankind was shown by illustrations drawn from the narrative of "the disciple whom Jesus loved." A profound yet simple examination of those conversations which Christ had with the people whom he met in public or in private served to emphasize the identity of human experiences in all ages and under all conditions.

In treating of the Prayer-Book this year, Dr. Brooks began by pointing out that, according to the fundamental conception of that book, the prayers are the people's prayers, and the Church belongs to the people, not to the clergy. Proceeding to unfold the meaning of forms grown familiar by constant use, attention was called to the foremost place which the doctrine of the Trinity occupies in the litany. This was declared to be an indication of the way in which the Church should regard all doctrine. " It is significant that not in her creeds, but in her prayers, the Church most clearly states her dogmas. It is significant that the Church holds her dogmas, not for their essential value, but for their uses. . . . But does it mean that you cannot pray until you can first utter these critical and test words? Is this great doctrine used as a sort of challenge at the doorway, so that souls who cannot thus believe in God shall feel that they cannot approach him? Surely not. . . . Let the soul pray, 'O God, if there be a God, come now and help me.' We recognize fully the most imperfect conception of God as a basis of prayer. But the richer and fuller the conception, the richer and fuller will the prayer be."

It is in this way that the Lenten lectures delivered from year to year in Trinity Church, Boston, are made so interesting, so helpful, so memorable, that vast throngs are always in attendance at their delivery, that whenever reported and published they are eagerly read in all parts of the country, and that their influence outreaches and outlasts the immediate occasion. The lectures are full of both doctrinal and practical theology, but always of the kind that springs with seeming spontaneity out of the theme and out of living present human interests.

.

SENTIMENT AND SENTIMENTALITY.

[July 17, 1888.]

In Dr. Brooks' wise and eloquent sermon preached in Trinity Church last Sunday morning before the National Prison-Reform Association a striking contrast was drawn between sentiment and sentimentality. The pulpit orator recognized it as an undoubted fact that the greatest obstacle in the way of the men and women who are seeking to make our prison management more humane is the popular idea that they are sentimentalists: whereas it is not sentimentality, but sentiment, which inspires them. "Sentiment," he said, "is fed straight out of the heart of truth: sentimentality is distorted by personal whims. Sentiment is active: sentimentality is lazy. Sentiment is self-sacrificing: sentimentality is self-indulgent. Sentiment loves facts: sentimentality hates them. Sentiment is clear-sighted: sentimentality is blind. In a word, sentiment is the health of nature, and sentimentality is its disease."

The distinction thus sharply drawn is too often overlooked, and is of vital importance. Exhibitions of sentimentality in connection with prisons and prisoners we have had *ad nauseam*. Its most disgusting features appear when some brutal wretch lies under sentence of death for unprovoked murder. The flowers sent to his cell, the dainty food, the rush to obtain his autograph, the heap of letters expressing tender interest which the postman brings him every morning, and the innumerable signatures attached to the petitions for pardon,— all this froth and slop of sentimentality are as familiar as they are discreditable. Even when the prisoner is not under capital sentence, there is more or less of the same sort of thing, the degree of folly exhibited being usually in proportion to the brutality of the crime.

Perhaps it is not strange, yet surely it is not necessary, that in many quarters the aims and methods of the National Prison-Reform Association should be confounded with such displays as we have alluded to. As Phillips Brooks says, "The great human sentiments are the only universal and perpetual powers." Sentiments of pity for the wretched and of sympathy with the

State in its efforts to repress and punish crime; sentiments which are full of justice, firmness and sternness, as well as full of charitableness,— do indeed underlie the self-sacrificing efforts of the Association over which ex-President Hayes presides. But with sentimentality these people have no part or lot.

PREACHING WITHOUT NOTES.

[Dec. 17, 1888.]

The Rev. Phillips Brooks, D.D., in the course of his "Lyman Beecher Lectures" at Yale College in 1876–77, said, addressing theological students, that it seemed to be expected that every man who undertook to give them advice would touch on the question whether or not the minister should use a manuscript in the pulpit; and that, for his part, he would say this : However true it might be that an extemporaneous sermon should receive the same care in preparation as one preached from manuscript, yet in actual fact it almost never did. On that ground Dr. Brooks emphatically expressed his preference for the written discourse. It is evident, however, that his opinion has undergone a change, and that, like Dr. Storrs, he is convinced that the manuscript in the pulpit is a hindrance, and not a help. More and more of late the famous rector of Trinity preaches extemporaneously, and that may now be said to be his usual practice. He may not have changed his opinion of years ago as to the likelihood that extemporaneousness will mean carelessness, but he manifestly takes pains that it shall mean no such thing in his pulpit. Dr. Brooks' torrent of unwritten speech comes pouring forth as accurate, as elegant, as compact, as it could be made by any labor of the pen.

PHILLIPS BROOKS' POWER.

[Dec. 26, 1888.]

It is impossible for any one who is present where Phillips Brooks speaks to avoid listening. He may not hear anything except a torrent of sounds and echoes; for that architectural masterpiece of Richardson, Trinity Church, is extremely defective, considered with reference to its acoustic properties. But, if a person is seated in such a place that the words of the speaker are audible, he will hear a great deal, and will give attention, whether he wants to or not. Many curious experiences have been narrated of strangers in Boston who have dropped into Trinity Church on a Sunday, not knowing or not caring that it contained the pulpit of a famous preacher, and who, when the sermon began, observing that the text was one on which they had heard a great many discourses, and that the preacher talked very rapidly, and not very distinctly, resolved not to listen. The conclusion of such narratives always is that the stranger presently found himself paying eager attention without having intended it or quite knowing how he came to do so.

Indeed, how he came to do so is one of the unsolved enigmas on which the students of such phenomena never tire of exercising their ingenuity. Of course, this does not mean that the fact itself is matter of surprise. That Phillips Brooks is interesting is just as obvious as that one of Turner's pictures is interesting. But why? Perhaps another Ruskin will some day arise to tell us.

Few great preachers have ever so baffled the critics as has Phillips Brooks. Beecher was, in the first place, a trained and skilled elocutionist. In the second place, he was almost supremely eloquent, in the common acceptation of the term. Spurgeon has the quality which manuals of rhetoric call "nervousness,"— a quality for which the common people have no name, but which the commonest as well as the most uncommon people profoundly feel when they encounter it in literature or oratory. Talmage is dramatic. Storrs' power was aptly, though but partially, indicated by Theodore Tilton a number of years ago, when, as editor of the *Independent*, he recommended Dr. Storrs to accept the call just extended him from a society worshipping in one of the most magnificent of Boston's churches; for, said Tilton, "how grandly he would fill it with the added pomp of his gorgeous words!" Moody is vividly colloquial. Joseph Parker of London is epigrammatic. Cannon Farrar illustrates his themes with historical pictures thrown, life-size, upon the screen from the stereopticon of his imagination. Professor Swing of Chicago is a prose poet.

No judicious critic would think to find the source of Phillips Brooks' power in any or all of the qualities above enumerated, though none of them, excepting skill in elocution, is wholly absent from Trinity pulpit. The failure of all attempts hitherto made in that direction is a warning, not to be lightly disregarded, against any new effort towards solving this complex enigma. Without being guilty of such rashness, one may nevertheless point out two manifest elements of that attraction which brings crowds to Trinity Church from week to week and from year to year.

Phillips Brooks is an "evangelical" preacher, in the true sense of that often perverted term. His Christmas sermon, reported in this morning's

Advertiser, is an evangelical sermon; that is, it sets forth with absolute fidelity the *evangelium*, the gospel story. That he believes what he preaches, and believes it to be infinitely important, no candid man doubts who hears him. It seems like a paradox, but it is true that many otherwise good sermons fail because there is not enough religion in them. From text to peroration one of Phillips Brooks' sermons is crowded with the spiritual food that men are hungering for, whether they know it or not.

No better illustration was probably ever furnished of Dr. Brooks' famous definition of a sermon —"the truth through personality"— than one of his own sermons. The whole man, physical and mental, moral and spiritual, preaches. Any true solution of the problem of the marvellous success which we have been considering must contain the converse of that apothegm which Phillips Brooks gave to the students of Yale College in 1876: "No man can do much for others who is not much himself."

WATCH-NIGHT MEETING.

[Jan. 1, 1889.]

Rev. Phillips Brooks is constantly furnishing in himself and his work illustrations of his own maxims. Probably this fact is susceptible of a two-fold explanation. He frames his maxims, as all profound maxims must be framed, out of the inner life of him who utters them ; and he is constantly striving to conform the actual to the ideal. For instance, one of his famous sayings is that Christianity steadily refuses to crystallize itself as the religion of any class or creed. And no better illustration of this saying can be found than a Trinity Church "watch-night" meeting.

Everybody has heard of Methodist and Second Adventist watch-night meetings; of the prayers, of the songs, the testimonies, the audible manifestations of religious enthusiasm with which members of these communions are accustomed in certain localities, and especially were accustomed in former times, "to watch the old year out and the new year in." The impression derived from witnessing or reading accounts of such gatherings naturally is that a watch-night service is peculiarly adapted to places and people where and among whom religious fervor is more highly esteemed than the graces of culture. Accordingly, the public devotional observance of the midnight hour between December 31 and January 1 is not extensively practised in New England. But, year after year, the wealthiest church in Boston, connected with that denomination which, of all Protestant communions, has the stateliest ceremonial of worship, celebrates "watch-night" with services so impressive, so solemn, so deeply spiritual, that the memory of them remains indelibly stamped upon the minds of many participants.

Last night, when the hour of eleven opened, Trinity Church appeared to be filled in every part: yet for some time afterward there was a constant stream of people entering and following the ushers, who kept on providing seats in all possible places until not another seat could be found; and then a multitude remained standing, until the last hour of 1888 was ended and the first hour of 1889 had come.

When two hymns had been sung and a brief service from the Prayer-Book was concluded,

Rev. Leighton Parks delivered a tenderly affectionate address on that scene of our Saviour's life where the people went out to meet him with palm-branches and hosannas. The application was to suggest how we are to go out to meet Christ during the coming year. "It may be," said Mr. Parks, "that you can only look into the coming year with fear and trembling. Let it come in any way it will, so only it enters into your heart, and enthrones itself in the spirit of love and undying faith. May we not go out to meet the king, simply willing to accept him as he comes?" At the conclusion of Mr. Parks' address another hymn was sung; and then Rev. Phillips Brooks spoke three or four minutes, urging home the thought that during every moment of the closing year God's hand has held and guided us, and that during the coming year we rest still more completely in his love, not because he loves us more, but because we may open our hearts wider to receive his love.

Then, as the hands of the clock that stood within the chancel-railing pointed to one minute of midnight, the great congregation bowed in silent prayer until twelve strokes had been sounded forth and 1889 had begun. The united repetition of the Lord's Prayer aloud ended this solemn stage of the service, after which Dr. Brooks again spoke a few earnest words, expressing the hope that all present might live stronger, purer, more manly, more womanly, more Christlike lives in the year that had begun than in the year that had closed.

THE DOCTRINE OF THE EPISCOPACY.

[Jan. 22, 1889.]

It is not true that Dr. Brooks "does not believe in episcopacy." At any rate, it is not true that he has ever said so or given any indication of such disbelief. No more is it true that the "Episcopal Church has always held, concerning the chief office in the sacred ministry," the extreme and exclusive sacerdotal views which Dr. Brooks opposes. Prof. George P. Fisher of Yale College showed, in his Dudleian lecture at Harvard some weeks ago, what was already known to all men learned in Church history, that in the beginning the Anglican church admitted the validity of non-episcopal ordination.

PHILLIPS BROOKS AND LYMAN ABBOTT.

[Nov. 11, 1889.]

Lyman Abbott, who preached last evening in
the chapel of Harvard University, and thus inau-
gurated his fortnight's term of service as chap-
lain in that institution, divides with Phillips
Brooks the honor of pre-eminence as a preacher
to studious young men. Both these distinguished
clergymen have a peculiar genius for so presenting Christian doctrine that it shall commend itself at once to the conscience and the reason.
The difficulties which modern scholarship en-
counters when asked to accept the creeds that
have long been held as standards of faith are
overcome in the teachings of Dr. Brooks and Dr.
Abbott, not by throwing away part of historical
Christianity or by appealing from reason to revelation, but by stripping religious truth of specu-
lative accretions and presenting it in original
simplicity, sublimity, and power. How to believe in Christianity and at the same time keep
an open mind for all the truths of science and

humanity that are coming to be seen in the light
of our times as never before, and how to make
all knowledge and all faith mutually helpful,—
this is what many a Harvard student must have
learned, or found guidance toward learning, last
evening in Appleton Chapel, as he gazed into the
luminous face and listened to the scholarly and
inspiring words of Henry Ward Beecher's successor.

EPISCOPAL SCHISM PREDICTED.

[March 11, 1890.]

A writer in Saturday's *Transcript*, who signs himself "C.," gives warning that the Protestant Episcopal Church is "approaching a crisis" because certain clergymen of that denomination recognize the ministerial standing of other clergymen not of that denomination. Although no names are mentioned, it is perfectly evident that "C." has in mind the most distinguished preacher in Boston, who is also the most distinguished preacher of the Protestant Episcopal Church of this country. If thumping hard words could annihilate an alleged heresiarch, even the towering form of Trinity's rector would vanish before the shower of verbal missiles fired at him. "Giving the lie to her laws,"—*i.e.*, the laws of the Church,— "lawlessness," "state of anarchy," "openly preach doctrines opposed to those of the Church," are some of the words and phrases that are employed against a man who is doing more every day to bring honor upon his Church than any dozen advocates of intolerance and sectarian arrogance have done in their whole lives.

As for the specific arguments that "C." employs to prove his charge of violating obligations to the Episcopal Church, a candid reader is almost compelled to believe that this heresy-hunter has been too busy looking after other men's supposed shortcomings ever to have studied the laws or history of the Church for which he assumes to speak. "Then are we in a most sorry state of discipline," cries this pruner in the Lord's vineyard," "when any single priest can, unrebuked by his diocesan (bishop), declare a man, not episcopally ordained, to be a minister of Christ; for that term should have but one meaning to him in view of his ordination vow." Now, the truth is, though "C." does not appear to be aware of it, that the Protestant Episcopal Church has never adopted any declaration which denies that any other ordination but its own is valid, or any rule of discipline which forbids its rectors to acknowledge the ministerial standing of clergymen belonging to other branches of the Universal Church. Moreover, it is matter of abundant historical record that many of the fathers and founders of the Church of England, including those most justly held in reverence, distinctly repudiated the notion, which has sprung up in certain quarters in later times, that no other than episcopal ordination can be efficacious. From the beginning until now there have been "Broad Churchmen," whether so called or not, who refuse to limit their faith to cast-iron creeds or their fellowship to sectarian and sacerdotal bounds. These names, from Hooker and Tillotson to Maurice, Robertson, Stanley, Chambers, Hall, and Phillips Brooks, have been and are stars in the Church's constellations of glory. " C.'s " argument from the "ordinal" would produce smiles if the subject were less sacred. It is declared in the ordinal that " these orders of ministers " — to wit, bishops, priests, and deacons — "have been from the Apostles' time." If the Church, in her Prayer-Book, insists upon the necessity of episcopal ordination, in order to the constituting a man a lawful bishop, priest, or deacon, is it not giving the lie to her laws when any individual priest recognizes a man not so ordained as a lawful minister? This is the gist of the accusation and plea for a verdict of guilty. As if one denomination might not lay down prin-

ciples for its own guidance without denying the
right of any other denomination to take a different view!

"C." is probably more alarmed or more ex-
pectant than there is occasion for him to be, if
he either fears or hopes, to use his own words,
"there will be a schism in this Church, the like
of which has never been seen." All the signs
point the other way. Schisms result from quar-
rels. It takes two parties to make a quarrel.
Broad Churchmen in the Episcopal Church will
not be one of the parties. They have no wish to
cast out their opponents. Their opponents have
no power to cast them out, and they will not
take themselves out. They are there to stay.

THE VACANT BISHOPRIC.

[April 1, 1891.]

In another column of to-day's *Advertiser* will
be found by far the fullest and most significant
presentation yet made public of Protestant Episcopal opinion in the diocese of Massachusetts
regarding the choice of a successor to the late
lamented Bishop Paddock. The ecclesiastical
polity of the denomination is such that the field
of choice is not limited by diocesan boundaries.
The episcopal chair may be filled by calling into
service a man who resides three thousand miles
away. It is by no means an uncommon thing
for possible candidates in a diocese to be passed
over, in order to place in the bishopric a prominent clergyman from a distant locality. But it
hardly needs to be said that, other things being
equal, almost any Churchman would rather have
a selection made out of home talent.

What adds a very special interest to the forth-
coming election to the bishopric of Massachusetts is the circumstance that a clergyman whom

probably universal sentiment pronounces to be
the most distinguished Protestant Episcopal rector in the United States already belongs to this
diocese. The wide-spread feeling that no other
name is so fit to be pronounced in this connection as that of Phillips Brooks, cannot cause surprise. It would indeed be matter for surprise if
such a feeling did not exist. It is not confined
to Massachusetts. It is safe to say that there is
not a city, village, or hamlet in the Union, where
Churchmen dwell, where the idea of Boston's far-
famed Trinity rector has not occurred as that
of the one man who might most naturally be
thought of to fill the vacant place.

The only cogent reason that can be rendered
against the choice of Dr. Brooks is based on
his very eminence. The pulpit from which he
preaches twice every Sunday to congregations
limited only by the capacity of the great church
is a throne of power. His qualifications as a
metropolitan preacher are surpassing and splendid. Is it not better, many people are asking,
that he continue to occupy his present place,
where not only his regular congregation, but multitudes of others, including strangers temporarily
sojourning in our city, can hear him, than that

the burdens of administrative routine be imposed
upon him, with the necessity of travelling from
church to church in the discharge of official functions? In short, there is no question about the
fitness of Phillips Brooks for the bishopric; but
there is felt to be some question about the fitness
of the bishopric for Phillips Brooks.

On the other hand, it is considered that the
position of chief pastor of the Protestant Episcopal Church in Massachusetts is an exalted one;
that it opens up vast and varied opportunities of
usefulness and influence; that, when occupied by
a man of national and international reputation, it
would at once become an immense factor in all
the councils of the Church assembled in national
convention; and, finally, that every parish in the
diocese — that is, in the Commonwealth — would
feel the mighty and quickening power of personal
contact with such eloquence, culture, and spiritual consecration as every parish needs and as is
not easy to find. Would Phillips Brooks accept
if elected? This question all are asking, but no
authoritative answer is to be expected until and
unless the situation becomes such that an answer
is officially called for. To say that he is not a
candidate in any sense whatever, otherwise than

as the loving admiration of the clergy and laity makes him the choice of a large element of the diocese, is but to say what all know who know the man. For knowledge beyond that we must await swiftly coming events.

A NON-PARTISAN BISHOP.

[April 24, 1891.]

There is one thing which every member, clerical or lay, of the Diocesan Convention soon to be held in Boston, ought to set his face like a flint against; and that thing is the drawing of party lines in the matter of choosing a successor to the late Bishop Paddock. Nothing else so robs an ecclesiastical election of its proper influence as partisanship. This is especially true regarding the election of a bishop; for, in order to command the respect due to his exalted position, it must be felt that he is the bishop of the whole Church, and not of a faction, great or small, within the Church. His functions are largely administrative, and in particular they are judicial. There is the same reason for removing the choice of a bishop from the belittling and embittering strife of party politics that there is for keeping the judicial ermine unspotted from such strife. For these reasons it would be a great calamity to the Protestant Episcopal Church in Massachusetts if the coming Convention should allow itself to be swayed in the discharge of its greatest duty by any appeals to factional watchwords, by any organization outside of the Church, seeking to rule the Church, and most especially by any secret caucus.

Human nature being what it is, there is great danger of this calamity, unless it be avoided by a general, spontaneous agreement to lay aside all divisions on minor issues, and unite, for the honor of the Church, upon some man so able, so famous, so imbued with spiritual fervor, so universally beloved inside and outside of the denomination, and, withal, so large-minded, that his election would not mean the victory of one section over another, but a common act for the common good.

No doubt there are times when this rule would be difficult to follow, because no man is available who has and is known to have these pre-eminent qualities. Happily there is at present a freedom from such difficulty. Within the diocese of Massachusetts is a clergyman who answers completely to this description. There was for a time much question whether or not he would consent to take the episcopate if it were offered him, no matter how urgently. The *Advertiser* was some time ago able to state on reliable authority that he would not refuse to obey the call of his brethren if it came to him in such a way as to make the path of duty plain. The movement for the choice of Phillips Brooks is in no way, shape, or sense a party movement. It is as far from that as the east is from the west. It is as strong with many who differ widely from his theological views as with those who agree most closely with him in respect to doctrine. The movement is unorganized because it is spontaneous. It is strong in its own proper strength, strong by reason of its reasonableness. It is not a "Low" Church movement, or a "Broad" Church movement, or a "High" Church movement. It is more than any one or all of them. It is a Church movement.

No mistake could well be greater than that of those who fear that, if Dr. Brooks were elected to the bishopric, he would show disfavor to such clergymen as might have adopted different ideas from those of the bishop regarding "apostolic succession," validity and efficacy of sacraments, ritualistic ceremonials, vestments, revision of the Prayer-Book, relation of the Protestant Episcopal Church to other Christian bodies, and such like matters. Dr. Brooks is too much of a man to be intolerant. The liberty he claims for himself he claims for others, and would be more than ready to grant to them. In short, he would not be the bishop of a part of the Church, but of the whole.

And what a bishop he would be! Inferior men, with little else to commend them, might indeed answer as candidates of this or that party; but the most distinguished clergyman of his denomination in the country is named for the vacant place solely because of his surpassing fitness.

"A NON-PARTISAN BISHOP."

[April 28, 1891.]

The *Advertiser* takes great pleasure in laying before its readers this morning a communication in advocacy of the election of Rev. Dr. Satterlee as Protestant Episcopal bishop of Massachusetts. Our correspondent is a layman who justly possesses in a high degree public confidence as a leader in professional and religious activities. There is no man in the diocese whose views at this juncture are entitled to receive greater attention.

No exception can be taken to anything that "Conservative" says in praise of his candidate's many admirable qualities of head and heart. Our own news columns of last Thursday contained equally extended and emphatic tributes of a similar nature.

It is therefore with unfeigned astonishment that we note the accusation that the *Advertiser* has made an attack on Dr. Satterlee's supporters. The editorial article in question was not intended as any such attack, either direct or indirect; nor did it contain any language which, by fair construction, as it seems to us, could be so interpreted. Dr. Satterlee's name was not mentioned. No allusion to him was made. Nothing was said about the fact of the selection of a candidate opposed to Phillips Brooks. No syllable of fault was found with those who, from whatever conscientious motives, prefer some man of less eminence than the Massachusetts divine whose name is arousing so much spontaneous enthusiasm among all schools of thought in the Church. The head and front of our offending consists in having uttered a warning on general grounds, in the interests of the Church as a whole, and without any criticism of any candidate or any candidate's friends, against the peril of making the choice of a bishop a party affair. We think our valued and courteous correspondent does unintentional injustice to the friends of Dr. Satterlee in seeming to say that an exhortation to unity, and to a laying aside of factional strife for the good and glory of a common cause, must be understood as aimed at that most excellent clergyman or at his adherents.

BISHOP PERRY'S LETTER.

[May 26, 1891.]

All signs point to the confirmation of Phillips Brooks by an overwhelming majority of votes. At the present writing the poll as reported stands twelve dioceses in favor and four against him. That is about the proportion which has been kept up since the contest began, and may fairly be taken as prophetic of the final result. The extraordinary demand that the bishop-elect of Massachusetts shall answer certain questions assumed to bear upon his fitness for episcopal office looks like a last effort of despair on the part of Dr. Brooks' opponents. They seem to see the tide running so strongly in his direction that they are fain to resort to means which almost irresistibly remind us once more of the broom with which "the excellent Mrs. Partington" attempted to beat back the Atlantic Ocean at Sidmouth.

Dr. Brooks is one of the most good-natured men alive. He is also one of the most compassionate. There is no doubt that he would be

only too glad to gratify the brethren who are in
so sore a plight if he could properly do so. But
he no doubt feels confident that even his most
zealous adversaries will, when their calmness is
restored, understand how entirely incompatible it
would be with the dignity of his position to sub-
mit to a course of catechising at this juncture.
It would inevitably be construed by those who
do not know him as an evidence of anxiety to
curry favor and win votes.

How absolutely unnecessary it is for him to go
upon the witness-stand and undergo cross-exami-
nation is perfectly plain to all concerned. If it
is not plain to Bishop Perry and the rector of the
Church of St. John the Evangelist in New York,
the reason must be that those devout brethren
have been so busy with other matters as to have
failed to keep pace with the most significant
developments in their own denomination. Dr.
Brooks has been for many years the foremost
preacher of the Protestant Episcopal Church in
America. He has been heard in his own pulpit
and other pulpits in many chief cities of the country by uncounted thousands of eagerly listening
auditors. He has preached and lectured extensively in Harvard and Yale, the leading Ameri-

can universities. He has been a leading contributor to leading newspapers and magazines. Numerous published and widely read volumes contain his matured thoughts on living questions in church and society. There is no mystery whatever about his attitude toward the very matters that he is asked to declare himself upon. He has declared himself once and again. Those, if there be such, who cannot understand what he has already said, could not understand what he might say. If what he has said needs explanation, any explanation would require to be explained, and so on indefinitely. Moreover, if he once began to answer questions, where would he stop? Every bishop and every member of every diocesan committee has an equal right to take a hand in the catechising. The whole idea is preposterous. It is irregular and uncanonical. There is provision made for examining by question and answer into the fitness of a theological student for ordination, but the rules of the Church recognize no such process for ascertaining the qualifications of a bishop-elect.

It must be remembered that Phillips Brooks has not sought the office. The office has sought Phillips Brooks. He was elected on his record.

On that record his election will stand or fall. The question for the Protestant Episcopal Church in America is simply this,— whether or not it will avail itself of the most splendid opportunity that has come in this generation for advancing its interests and enhancing its honor. The fame and influence of the bishop-elect are beyond the reach of envy or bigotry. The episcopal office cannot add anything thereto, but may receive much therefrom.

There is one part of Bishop Perry's extraordinary letter, if possible, the most extraordinary of all. It is that part in which he seems to demand that Dr. Brooks give certain "assurances" and express certain "regrets." We forbear using in regard to this such plainness of speech as would find instant response in the hearts of thousands and tens of thousands who respect others because they respect themselves. There may possibly be clergymen who would renounce their convictions and repudiate their utterances for the sake of a bishopric, though we would not willingly believe it. We feel an assurance that, when Bishop Perry becomes acquainted with Bishop Brooks, the latter will receive from the former proper expressions of regret.

BISHOPS' VOTE NEXT.

[June 6, 1891.]

The most universally interesting single item of news in yesterday's papers was that a majority of the standing committees, representing twenty-seven out of fifty-two dioceses of the Protestant Episcopal Church in the United States, had voted in favor of confirming Phillips Brooks' election as bishop of Massachusetts. There has never been another such instance of public interest in a matter of this kind. A good many people seem to be puzzled to understand why so very marked an exception is made in this case; why a question which can be decided only by a limited number of official votes, representing a single religious organization, is made to seem like a great public question dependent upon universal suffrage. Particularly does the share taken by leading metropolitan newspapers in the case perplex certain well-meaning folk. These folk hardly know whether to be glad or sorry, pleased or displeased; but of one thing they are sure, and that is that they are surprised.

Yet it is all very plain. The public is widely
interested in whatever is widely interesting. The
choice of a denominational officer is commonly
of no vital concern to the sect which makes the
choice, and of none at all outside of that sect.
This is true, whether the position to be filled
is that of bishop in the Protestant Episcopal
Church, presiding elder in the Methodist Episcopal Church, president of the Presbyterian General Assembly, moderator of a Congregational
council, or any similar place. There is a certain
ecclesiastical machinery to be kept in motion;
and provision must be duly made for attending
to the wheels, cogs, belts, and shafting. Very
often there is nothing that can be properly called
election or selection. Five sentences exhaust
the topic in discussion, and five lines are ample
for the announcement of results.

In the case of Phillips Brooks and the Massachusetts bishopric all this is changed. All sorts
of reasons exist for the large space which the
subject occupies in current speech and print. It
is not merely the eminence, the pre-eminence, of
the man. It is not the peculiarly influential
character of the diocese. It is not the opposi-
tion that has been aroused. It is not any excep-

tional acceptability of the bishop-elect's doctrinal views. These have something to do with it; but not half so much as is imagined. There are far deeper, more potent reasons for the public interest. The election of Phillips Brooks to the bishopric is of universal interest, because it signifies that positive rather than negative qualities are sought. It means that the man is to adorn the office, not the office the man. It means that partisanship is at a discount, and personality at a premium. It means that essentials are regarded more than incidentals. The general public care extremely little about distinctions of " High " and " Low " and " Broad " Church ; but it is closely touched by whatever affects the rights of free speech and untrammelled thought in Church or State. The questions at issue in this episcopal campaign are parallel with questions that are all the time at issue in every religious sect, every political party, every school of literature, art, or science, every line of life. Therefore, it is felt that the outcome of this contest will serve as a kind of mile-stone to mark the progress of mankind along certain paths that lead to better things for us all. Looked at in this light, it is easy to see why the question of Phillips Brooks' confirmation takes its place among the leading topics of the day, and especially why the foremost daily newspapers give it reportorial and editorial prominence.

It now remains for the bishops to add their sanction. It is to be taken for granted that this will not be long delayed. To suppose that any considerable number of them will try or desire to thwart the expressed wishes of the diocese of Massachusetts and of a majority of the standing committees representing dioceses throughout the country would be to do the reverend prelates great injustice. On the contrary, it is more courteous to them, and more reasonable, to assume that a large majority of the bishops will hasten to signify the pleasure with which they are prepared to welcome so noble an associate.

IT WILL BE BISHOP BROOKS.

[July 13, 1891.]

Congratulations to the bishops of the Protestant Episcopal Church in the United States! By their action in giving sanction to the choice of Phillips Brooks they have done the greatest possible thing to enhance the esteem in which they are personally and officially held by Christian America. Henceforth it will be everywhere understood that the foremost clergyman in each diocese is none too eminent for its titular headship. It will be presumed that the same principles which governed the choice of a bishop in Massachusetts were applied when each of the other threescore elections to similar offices were held. If any one shall venture in the future to suggest that breadth of view, nobleness of spirit, true catholicity, are qualities conspicuous by their absence from the house of bishops, the aspersion will be instantly met by triumphant reference to the splendid enthusiasm with which a man whose name is a synonyme for all these, as well as for transcendent spiritual and mental gifts, was made a member of that house by all the authorities having responsibility in the matter, including the reverend prelates whose associate he was to become. The bishops are to be congratulated, not only on the credit which will accrue from their affirmative votes, but on a happy escape from the very serious loss of prestige which a contrary course of action must have entailed.

It is in order once again to point out how far removed the choice of Phillips Brooks to be bishop of Massachusetts is from a party victory. The *Advertiser* has from the first placed emphasis upon this idea. His defeat would have meant the assertion of partisanship: his success means its rebuke. He stands for the Church and the whole Church, for the Church in the very truest and largest sense of the word. It is perhaps inevitable that party questions must arise in connection with so vital a decision as that by which an episcopal vacancy is filled. There are three ways of meeting the issue. One is by drawing party lines and forcing the minority to the wall. The second is by evasion and compromise. The third is by rising above partisanship, and choosing on grounds so high that lower motives are left out of sight. Who can doubt that the third way is the best? Who that wishes well to the Church can fail to rejoice that the best way was adopted in this instance?

The long uncertainty is at last ended. The right, the wise, the fitting thing is assured. Nothing but the ceremonies of consecration remain to be performed, in order that the man whom American Christianity delights to honor because he is an honor to American Christianity may take the place for which he is so eminently, so pre-eminently, fitted by nature and grace. Now may all that has marred the fraternity of religious brotherhood be forgotten, and only that remembered of which the memory will serve to promote the interests which all worthy followers of the great head of the Universal Church have at heart.

"BISHOP OF MASSACHUSETTS."

[July 18, 1891.]

A gentleman residing in this city, who is well known among literary people, has written a personal letter to the editor of the *Advertiser*, suggesting that, in view of the great public interest felt in the election and approaching confirmation of Phillips Brooks as bishop of the Protestant Episcopal Church in Massachusetts, it might be well to point out an error of expression which, for the sake of verbal exactness, should be avoided. Objection is taken to the term "Bishop of Massachusetts," on the ground that in a country which has no State Church there is and can be no such ecclesiastical functionary; that, however proper in England may be the title, "Bishop of London," "Bishop of Durham," "Bishop of Exeter," in America there is no "Bishop of Iowa," and the prelatical head of a particular Christian denomination in this Puritan Commonwealth, though he be never so honored and beloved by the people regardless of creed or church, ought not to be styled "Bishop of Massachusetts."

As a matter of strict accuracy, there is no disputing these propositions. Moreover, they relate to a truth that every American citizen should fully understand,— a truth which may with great propriety be emphasized at this time, when public attention is likely to be more readily fixed upon it than would be possible ordinarily. The *Advertiser* has been careful to avoid giving countenance to any mistake or confusion of the kind that our correspondent deprecates. In commenting on the auspicious outcome of the diocesan convention's vote for bishop, we said, in substance, that by reason of his breadth of view and fellowship, which overleap all sectarian lines, yet with perfect loyalty to his own branch of the Universal Church, Phillips Brooks would not only be the bishop of the Protestant Episcopal Church in Massachusetts, but in some real and complete sense the bishop of Massachusetts. No reader could have failed to understand the purport of the closing expression as containing a careful distinction between an official bishopric and one that is wholly derived from personal worth, recognized by admiring affection.

It seems to us, nevertheless, that it may be possible to use the term in question without qualification, yet without confusion or real inexactness. It is a law of language, with which no one is better acquainted than our correspondent, that any term is limited in meaning by the known limits within which it is used. In speaking of the late gubernatorial convention in Ohio, we do not need always to specify whether we mean the one that nominated Major McKinley or the one that renominated Governor Campbell. So "the Bishop of Massachusetts" might mean Bishop Williams of the Roman Catholic Church, and would be so understood if matters affecting that church were under discussion. In like manner any clergyman may be mentioned as pastor of the "church" in a particular locality, although, as a matter of fact, there are several churches there of as many denominations, "the church" being understood to signify the Baptist, Congregational, Methodist Episcopal, Protestant Episcopal, or any other church, according to the known denominational relations of the clergyman.

There is the less danger of any misunderstanding with reference to the term "Bishop of

Massachusetts," because he who is soon to become bishop of the Protestant Episcopal Church of Massachusetts cannot even be imagined, by any one who knows him, as claiming the former title in any arrogant or exclusive sense.

PHILLIPS BROOKS' SERMON.

[Oct. 12, 1891.]

There was "standing-room only " in Trinity
Church yesterday afternoon when the service
opened at which the bishop-elect of the Protestant Episcopal Church of Massachusetts preached
his last sermon as rector of the parish of which
he has been the honored head for more than
twenty years. The lowering clouds and fitful
rain had no effect to deter the surging throngs
who were eager for one more chance to listen to
the words of life from those eloquent lips ere he
whom they had so long known and loved as Phillips Brooks should become Bishop Brooks.

It would be inexact to speak of the discourse
as a "farewell sermon." The case was far different from that where a clergyman bids adieu to
his people, and is about to go hence to assume
toward another flock relations similar to those
which are being severed. Although Trinity
Church has displayed a noble unselfishness in
giving up without protest a prize which any con-

gregation of worshippers in the world might be
proud to possess, yet it is not to be for a moment
supposed that the sacrifice is at all such as would
have been involved, had the society acquiesced
in his acceptance of a "call" to another local
pastorate. Boston will still be the great preacher's home, and it cannot be, ought not to be, otherwise than that he will always recognize some
special ties of love and service binding him to
the place and people that have been so inti-
mately connected with his life hitherto. It may
have been on account of feeling this that no direct allusion was made yesterday afternoon to
any approaching separation. At the same time
there was a very marked and special significance
in the tenderly solemn and affectionate words
spoken in the pulpit, which can never again be
exactly the same pulpit that it has been so long.

The text itself was strikingly appropriate,
being from the last chapter of the Book of Revelation, therefore among the final and farewell
words of the Bible: "And the Spirit and the
Bride say, Come. And let him that heareth say,
Come. And let him that is athirst come. And
whosoever will, let him take the water of life
freely."

To those who are acquainted with Phillips
Brooks' fundamental conceptions of Christian
truth, and who had the inestimable privilege of
listening to this sermon, it must have been evident that the preacher designed to sum up once
more, in simple, earnest, impassioned pleadings,
the lessons which it has been the task of his ministry to teach.   Beginning with a reference to
the element of finality in the text, a recognition
of the words as containing a farewell, the preacher
called attention to the fact that they point on-
ward and upward.   They are full of the future.
The better, brighter, broader day that must come
for the Church, for the world, and for each human
life that attains its true destiny, was the thought
set forth, under that head, as only such a theme
can be set forth by such a man.

Then, as the culminating message, came the
doctrine which constitutes the central sun of
Phillips Brooks' preaching, of which he never
tires, of which his hearers never tire, of which,
we may be rejoicingly sure, the people in the
larger ministry upon which he is about to enter
will never tire,— the doctrine that Christianity, in
its heart of hearts, is not a creed, not a cere-
mony, not a law, but is a person, is the living,

loving, present person, who was born in Bethlehem, died on Calvary, and is never very far from every one of us. It is such teaching as this which the world needs, and which will, without a doubt, make the ministry of Bishop Brooks even more fruitful, if that be possible, than the ministry of Phillips Brooks has been.

BISHOP BROOKS' CONSECRATION.

[Oct. 15, 1891.]

Regarding the solemnly impressive yet joy-inspiring services in Trinity Church yesterday morning it is not possible for any human language to express adequately the thoughts and emotions that rise in uncounted multitudes of deeply stirred hearts. The elaborate ceremonial was all that it could be, moving on from first to last in simple grandeur according to the order of the church for such occasions made and provided. The place of consecration was itself an essential element, contributing no small share to the sacred splendors of the scene. We do not mean merely that the edifice within whose walls Phillips Brooks received the vestments of a bishop was of all churches in this Commonwealth most fitting by reason of its architectural magnificence, though that is true. But the rudest tabernacle ever constructed out of rough-hewn timbers would have been hardly less fit if it had been, as Trinity Church has been, the meeting-place for many a year of hungry throngs to whom our peerless preacher was wont to break the bread of life. Nothing was absent that could give dignity and grace and memorableness,—neither pulpit oratory, nor appropriate music, nor stately pageantry, nor presence of distinguished men, nor participation of eminent prelates, nor long lines of white-robed priests, nor an audience rapt in eager attentiveness, limited in numbers only by the inexorable limitations of space. Yet this was not all. There were few, if any, who yesterday had the never-to-be-forgotten privilege of witnessing the spectacle beneath the majestic tower of Trinity who did not realize that the vast and sympathetic assemblage gathered there was but an infinitesimal fraction of the mighty mass of people outside who were there in spirit, who would seize the earliest opportunity to read of what had there taken place, and whose souls would unite in response to the voices that said "Amen!" when divine blessings were invoked upon the newly made bishop.

No one in the American Church could have been chosen more suitable than Bishop Potter of New York for the great office of preacher at such a time. As yet the title of archbishop is un-

known to the Protestant Episcopal denomination
on this side the ocean. Whether it is well that
this is so has been questioned of late. Opinion
differs as to that; but it is probable that no one
would dispute the statement that, if yesterday
morning the suffrages of the Church could have
been taken as to the one among all living members of the episcopate best entitled by learning
and by gifts of nature and grace to be chosen to
exercise arch-episcopal functions, a majority of
ballots would have been cast for Henry C. Potter. If such a vote were to be taken to-day, and
should result otherwise, it could only be for the
reason that another great name has been added
to the roll of the house of bishops. The discourse preached from Trinity pulpit yesterday
was throughout worthy of the preacher and the
occasion. It was logical, eloquent, and scholarly.
It was such as the whole country has learned to
expect from Bishop Potter. It was loyal to the
Church of which the prelate is a distinguished
ornament, at the same time that it was catholic
in recognition of the Church Universal. But we
do not in the least disparage other portions when
we say that the crowning interest of the sermon
attaches to that portion which was devoted to

the personality toward which all hearts turned.
They were brave, strong, generous, tender, noble
words of welcome that the great bishop addressed to the great bishop-elect. Their bearing
is not confined to their immediate application.
They contain truths which the whole Protestant
Episcopal Church will do well to heed and remember. If, together with a fervent personal
tribute to the pre-eminent worthiness of the individual, to whom they were addressed, to hold the
highest office in the gift of the Church, there was
mingled something of indignant rebuke of the
spirit that would have forbidden the Church to
choose for one of its bishops "the man who has
the widest vision and the largest love," who can
deny, remembering what we would all fain for-
get, that the rebuke was needed? For the honor
of the Church let us hope that a similar rebuke
will never be needed again. The universal interest that has for months been felt in the election, confirmation, and now in the consecration
of Phillips Brooks to be bishop of the Protestant
Episcopal diocese of Massachusetts, is something
phenomenal. We need not wonder that it causes
wonder. It is indeed wonderful. Nothing like
it was ever known in America before. The topic

rivals in the public mind all other current themes.
An exciting political campaign is not more talked
about, certainly not among thoughtful citizens.
Foreign news, big with the fate of governments
and touching on problems of war and peace
among nations, stirs not intelligent readers more
profoundly.   Whoever would understand this
phenomenon must look for reasons beyond all
sectarian lines and all ordinary personal factors.
It is because Phillips Brooks that was, the
Bishop Brooks that is and is to be, has endeared
himself to a circle wider than any denomination,
than all denominations.   What the preacher indicated yesterday is true.   We honor him who is
consecrated, not chiefly for his eloquence, his
learning, his achievements as pastor of a great
church, or even for his noble services as a foremost citizen, ready to speak potent words on be-
half of every worthy cause within the city and
the Commonwealth.   It would come nearer the
secret to say that it is his Christian character,
tried by many tests and never found wanting,
that commands our homage.   But something
more must be said before the story is told.

Bishop Brooks occupies a place in the hearts
of men that can only be described by using the

word "gratitude." He has done for tens of thousands an inestimable service. He has taught us, not only how to die, but how to live. He has unravelled for us the solemn mysteries of man's mission "on this bank and shoal of time." He has made the fatherhood of God seem real. He has made religion seem a privilege, and daily communion with divine nature a possibility. He has helped us to believe in better things than we had known before. He has touched hidden and unsuspected springs of high ambition. Life, to uncounted multitudes, appears more worth living because of the instruction, the inspiration, the example of him whom henceforth we shall delight to call Bishop Brooks. Therefore, we unfeignedly thank him, and rejoice with all those who do rejoice in the consecration to the bishopric of this already consecrated man.

HELEN KELLER'S THOUGHT OF GOD.*

[Jan. 7, 1892.]

The story which we publish this morning of how little Helen Keller, the blind child whose education at the Perkins Institute has attracted — and rewarded — so much notice, came to a knowledge of God, is one of the sweetest and sublimest narratives ever brought out in this world. Whatever our readers neglect in to-day's *Advertiser*, we hope none of them will fail to read this story. For old and young, for religious and irreligious people alike, it is exceedingly valuable. And to say that it is interesting is but a feeble statement. It is of absorbing interest. Indeed, so touching, tender and thrilling, so full of new light on a problem that never grows old is it, that we have little fear that any one who begins to read will cease before reaching the last word.

Helen Keller's experience is a revelation in child-nature. It shows that, even under conditions of apparently supreme difficulty, and when

* See Appendix.

left almost alone to the humanly unaided struggles of her own mind and heart after infinite truth, this little blind girl reached a crisis where the hunger for knowledge concerning God prompted her to call on the dearest friends she knew to teach her. It is but a little while since a good deal was said in Boston about the trial of an experiment to find out whether or not elementary religious ideas are in any sense innate. It would seem as though such a question need no longer be asked.

It is occasion for rejoicing that the first instruction that she was able to comprehend, in religious doctrine, was given by one so wise and in every way fit for the heavenly task as Bishop Phillips Brooks. Would that every child — yea, and every grown person, too — might be taught by him that creed, which is better than all the churches' confessions and catechisms, " God is love "!

CHRIST IN BOSTON.

[March 15, 1892.]

One of the most striking passages in Bishop
Brooks' Lenten lecture in St. Paul's Church yesterday was the eloquent picture of the effect that
might be expected to result from a bodily visit of
the Lord Jesus Christ to Boston.   The theme is
a familiar one.   Preachers and newspapers often
attempt such a picture, but they generally repre-
sent the people as indifferent or scornful toward
the wonderful visitant.   Phillips Brooks takes a
much wiser view.   He thinks that, if Jesus were
to walk down State Street or enter an abode of
wealth and fashion on Beacon Hill, a hush would
instantly fall upon the noisy scenes of specula-
tion, a sense of uplifting presence would come to
gay throngs, men would want to stop their base
dealings, women would become ashamed of their
frivolous lives.   And, when we come to think
of it, is not this the more reasonable picture?
Something very like that was what took place in
the first century in Jerusalem.   Surely, after the

lapse of eighteen hundred years, during which the Christ-idea has been working in the world, it might fairly be expected that at least an equal welcome would await the world's spiritual Master if he were to make a visible appearance in the nineteenth century in Boston.

REACHING THE MASSES.

[Nov. 12, 1892.]

It is a fundamental error to think that he who would raise the fallen must put himself upon their level in language, in dress, or in deportment. A few years ago Phillips Brooks preached a series of sermons in Faneuil Hall on Sunday evenings, and was heard by throngs of such people as the Christian Workers' Convention leaders are trying to reach. He did not let himself down : he did draw them up. His Faneuil Hall sermons were in style and every other essential respect similar to his Trinity Church sermons. Yet he was heard by one audience as attentively as by the other. A still greater example can be cited. There was once a preacher in Jerusalem who did city missionary work, whom beggars and lepers and thieves and women who were sinners crowded to hear, whose converts were mainly poor, who scarcely numbered a single member of the city's four hundred among his parishioners. But he never mistook levelling down for levelling up. He was the most perfect gentleman that ever lived. He was as full of dignity as of sympathy and gentleness. He did not talk slang. And "the common people heard him gladly."

THE GREAT GRIEF.

[Jan. 24, 1893.]

The first and strongest impression produced on countless multitudes of people yesterday when they received the startling tidings of Bishop Brooks' death was one of personal sorrow, intensified by the terrible shock that its entire unexpectedness caused. It is not possible to put into words the depth and strength of this feeling. It is an experience that seldom comes to a community, for the men are extremely rare who can inspire it. Very often, indeed, the death of a famous, honored and influential citizen becomes the chief topic for a time in extended circles, he is sincerely lamented and his loss is profoundly realized. But nearly always, in such a case, the sense of personal bereavement is confined within limits vastly narrower than circumscribe the recognition of distinguished and departed worth. The extraordinary individual for whom we mourn at this time was gifted even more wonderfully with the qualities that inspire reverent affection than with those other characteristics that he possessed in no common measure, yet shared with mental and moral greatness wherever found. This death has brought heart-ache to more lives than he who was so humble amid his clustering honors can ever have anticipated, to more lives than any one but the recording angel can enumerate.

It is at this point that so many attempts to explain the secret of his power over human kind break down. The bottom of the mystery lies in the perfect confidence which men and women and children felt in his goodness. That last word seems inadequate, merely because it is so often used as the antithesis of greatness, whereas, in describing Phillips Brooks, the two words belong together. No one could separate them without failing to express the truth. The man was good and great, great and good; but the impression produced by a slight knowledge of him, and increased with increasing knowledge that has been growing with the growth of his years and widening of his influence, is that his goodness was the rarer and more precious quality of the two. The predominant impulse that Phillips Brooks awakened was not to admire his bril-

liant talents. It was a longing to become a par-
taker in his lofty faith and to pattern after his
superb character.

Probably there never was an example of eloquence, whether displayed in the pulpit, at the
bar, on the lecture-platform, or in legislative
halls, that was at once more universally acknowl-
edged or more difficult to account for than that
of the ex-rector of Trinity Church. Certainly he
displayed few of the usual resources of oratory.
His vocal defects were marked and at times
painful to himself and to his auditors. His language was hardly ever ornate. In the sense in
which the phrase is commonly used, he was not a
"prose poet." He made very sparing use of "illustrations" drawn either from external Nature
or from history, literature, or art; though his oc-
casional metaphors were surprisingly apt, pure
gems in perfect setting. There were seldom passages in his sermons that were of such exceptional brilliancy as to stand out in memory apart
from the body of the discourse. In that as in
many other respects he differed from the great
preacher with whom alone of modern American
pulpiteers he can be compared, the late Henry
Ward Beecher. Hence Bishop Brooks' elo-

quence endures less than that of most famous
orators the test of brief extracts. "The Beau-
ties of Ruskin" is the title given to a book of se-
lections that does no injustice to the great critic,
but any attempt to exhibit the genius of Bishop
Brooks by such a method can never be suc-
cessful.

His eloquence consists in matter rather than
manner. It has been said, "The style is the
man." This is not true in the instance now
under consideration. Instead we must say,
"The man was the style." The whole man —
body, brain, and soul — was eloquent. Words,
thoughts, emotions, tones, the towering and elec-
trifying physical presence, the great, deep-set,
flashing eyes, the moral majesty back of everything,— it was the combination of all these things
that made up the sum of the eloquence that
stirred and swayed vast audiences.

Great orators, poets in prose or verse, have
generally depended largely upon the spell
wrought by word-picturings of the sublime and
beautiful in Nature; by presenting to the mind's
eye stars, flowers, forests, mountains, limpid
streams, cataracts, the ocean in storm and calm.
Phillips Brooks knew the human soul as Thoreau

knew the New England woods, and Tennyson the castle walls of Old England. He revealed the wonderland of love. He painted to throbbing hearts the aspirations of mortals for immortality. He bade men look up and look forth at the dignity and the worth of human life. He was eloquent in portrayal of forgotten possibilities. Common thoughts, familiar truths, old doctrines worn threadbare by ages of stereotyped repetition, passing through the alembic of his great soul, emerged in splendor; and men and women of the world, grown callous by worldliness, were strangely moved at hearing anew from his lips the gospel story that they had learned at their mother's knee, but had well-nigh forgotten for many and many a year.

There was one feature of Dr. Brooks' preaching that was especially characteristic, and that can be more clearly defined than some others. We allude to his constant habit of philosophical analysis. The very word "analysis" seems to suggest something "dry," formal, scholastic; more suitable for the college lecture-room than for the pulpit. But his analysis was as unlike common men's as was all else that he was or did. It would be worth the pains for any one

who is desirous to learn the secret of his power
to study this feature. Everybody who heard him
was wont to exclaim upon the "freshness" with
which familiar ideas were set forth. Very often
that consisted in showing how what seems to be
simple is really complex; how unity is full of va-
riety; how a moss-grown trunk of truth is but
the beginning and basis of a noble tree that
reaches toward heaven, that stretches its giant
arms far and wide, that is beautiful with foliage
and bountiful in fruitage, and in whose branches
the birds of the air lodge and sing.

Phillips Brooks was one of the most accom-
plished of scholars. The multitude did not fully
appreciate this fact, for the reason that he made
no display of his rich resources. Pedantry was
his abomination. People did not think of calling
him a learned man. Yet there was no field of intellectual cultivation to which he was a stranger.
His culture was of the finest, his tastes of the
purest. "No man can do much for others who
is not much himself," was a maxim he laid down
in his "Lyman Beecher Lectures" before the
divinity students of Yale College, sixteen years
ago. That maxim supplies the key to one treas-
ure-chamber of his career. He was much him-

self; and by a lifetime of the highest study, for which he found or made leisure in the midst of incessant public activities, he was always adding to his marvellous store of the best knowledge.

The influence which he exerted in Boston, the city of his love, the city where the greatest portion of his active life was spent and his career culminated and concluded, was something of which it would hardly be possible to speak in exaggerated terms. Since the death of Wendell Phillips no citizen of our city has been so pre-eminently its representative, unless we except Oliver Wendell Holmes and Edward Everett Hale. Certainly, no orator whosoever has in these later years been so eagerly heard by our people at home, or has uttered with such commanding effect the city's noblest thought abroad. His position in Boston suggests comparison with that of Savonarola in Florence, of Luther in Wittenberg, of Calvin in Geneva, and of Bossuet in Paris. But, for the most striking parallel, we must revert to the history of the fourth Christian century, and recall the name and fame of Chrysostom, "the golden-mouth," Bishop of Constantinople.

A TEACHER OF THEOLOGY.

[Jan. 25, 1893.]

There are so many lessons to be learned from
Phillips Brooks' life that some of the most useful
of them are in danger of being overlooked at this
time when impressions concerning that wonderful man are, to an exceptional extent, undergoing
the creative and recreative process. Among the
many appreciative tributes which appeared in the
newspapers, yesterday, there was a notable lack,
so far as our observation reached, of any ade-
quate recognition of his influence as a theological teacher. This omission is not strange. He
was almost as far as possible from being a theo-
logian in the accepted sense of the term. It is
questionable whether, in the whole course of his
ministry, he ever preached what is called a doctrinal sermon. It is certain that he never entered the lists of theological disputation either
as an author of books or a writer of polemical
essays for magazines and church periodicals. It
is quite likely that some intelligent people, who

often heard him preach, would not be able to-day
to give even a brief outline of his opinions on
the doctrinal questions most debated at the present time. It is more than quite likely that one
might have heard him preach a score of times
without being able to gain from the sermons
themselves so much as a hint as to whether Dr.
Brooks was an Episcopalian, a Congregationalist,
a Baptist, or member of some other Christian
sect. Yet no preacher was ever more positive
in conviction or courageous in utterance.

Furthermore, those who are in a position to
judge from the inside as well as the outside have
long realized that the extraordinary man for
whom English - speaking Christendom mourns
was making an impress upon the doctrinal
thought of the closing years of the century that
could not fail to powerfully affect the trend of
creed-revision in the twentieth century. The
masses of people failed to perceive this, except
possibly in a vague way, because they were so accustomed to hear theological discussions carried
on by the processes of attack and defence, of
assertion and denial, of arguments pro and con.
Here was a man who never argued, though he
was forever reasoning; who was positive without

being pugnacious; whose sermons were richly Biblical, but were free from "proof-texts." So people scarcely thought of him as a leader of credal movements. Perhaps no one feature of Dr. Brooks' remarkable career is more instructive than this,— the way he taught people more reasonable and Christ-like doctrines than narrower teachers had formulated, yet never seemed to be at all concerned with controversial theology.

His method was to put the new truth in place of the old error; and, without making any fuss about it, without turning aside from his main work by one hair's breadth to answer objections or win consent, just to go on and use the new truth for religious purposes, and use it so vigorously, so luminously, with such inspiring spirituality, that everybody who noticed the absence of the old idea would feel how very much better the new was.

A single instance will illustrate our meaning. A number of years ago Phillips Brooks delivered, during the Lenten season, a series of Friday-afternoon lectures in Trinity Church on the Psalms of David. One day he took up what are known as "the imprecatory psalms,"— those in which King David calls upon God to send down all manner of evils upon the king's enemies, and even upon their little children. The question of how these psalms ought to be regarded is one that has long troubled devout people. Of course, the traditional view is that David was inspired from Heaven to utter these dreadful imprecations, and that somehow we must believe that they just as truly express the divine mind as does Christ's prayer upon the cross for his murderers, " Father, forgive them, for they know not what they do." But many and many a tender, loving, worshipping heart has found that interpretation a terrible stumbling-block. The rector of Trinity did not waste a word in arguing against the old view : he simply alluded to it as one that stood in the way of faith, then described the imprecatory psalms as specimens, which God had preserved for mankind's instruction, of the horrible wickedness into which even a worshipper of God, a man who tried to be a servant of God, was liable to fall if he did not watch and pray against his besetting temptation. Moreover, the preacher used these psalms as a most striking illustration of the elementary stage in religious character that the best of the patriarchs and other Old Testament worthies had been able to reach without a knowledge of Christ, contrasting that with the immeasurably loftier plane set before us in the New Testament.

Thus a portion of Scripture that by false interpretation had been made a sore hindrance to faith was by a truer interpretation rendered beautiful and helpful. At the same time a vitally important principle of Scriptural exegesis was introduced,—a principle that is closely connected with some of the questions at issue in the Andover case and the Briggs case. Leaders of progressive religious thought can learn a great deal by closely studying the methods of the great Broad Churchman, whose loss all kinds of churchmen and Christians of every name deplore.

THE LAST OF EARTH.

[Jan. 27, 1893.]

Yesterday Boston witnessed and participated in the greatest, most impressive, most instructive funeral-service that this city has known for many and many a year. No description can do justice to its solemn grandeur, no teachings adequately unfold its deep and lofty lessons. Our people are not unfamiliar with the pageantry of "obsequious sorrow." Sometimes they have seen high civic officials committed to their last resting-place, accompanied by whatever stately ceremonials can testify to the appreciation of public worth, and give dignity to the sad honors which the living pay to the memory of the dead. Again they have been spectators of the majestic rites with which illustrious soldiers are laid away in the tomb where silence and eternal peace take the place of war's alarms. He, whom Boston buried yesterday, was neither statesman nor military commander. He had held no civic office, had achieved no material glory. He was a sim-

ple citizen of the nation, the Commonwealth, and
the city; in that respect no more or less than
each of the thousands upon thousands who gathered in the beautiful temple so closely associated
with his name, or thronged in the spacious square
in front, in order that, if it were possible, they
might gain one more glimpse of that beloved
face, or, failing in that, join their voices in the
hymn to be sung out of doors,—"O God, our
help in ages past!"—and bow their heads and
weep when the great preacher should pass for
the last time out of the sanctuary, whose consecrated walls had so often echoed to the sound of
his voice in sermon and in prayer. He was only
a citizen, as were the countless multitudes who,
compelled by the day's duties to remain away
from those sacred scenes, no less sincerely
mourned an irreparable loss.

The sublimity of the tribute paid by the people of Boston to the memory of Phillips Brooks
was in its simplicity. That is true of the tribute
which is true of him in whose honor it was rendered. And the circumstances show how safe and
wise a thing it is to heed the throbbings of the
popular heart, when stirred by grand impulses.
It was the people who were quickest to discern

the incomparable worth of Phillips Brooks. They
knew him, flocked to him, loved and trusted him.
A good deal was said a couple of years ago about
the public voice that almost with one accord
named him as the proper successor to the
lamented Bishop Paddock. Something was now
and then said in ecclesiastical and sacerdotal
quarters in a tone of impatience, even of resent-
ment, regarding this public voice, especially as
it found utterance in the newspapers. As though
the question, being exclusively one for a single
sect, if not a section of a sect, to decide, any expression of the popular mind about it was little
less than an impertinence! Later it was reproach-
fully asserted that the miscellaneous people, and
especially their exponents, the newspapers, had
made Phillips Brooks bishop. There was a certain measure, greater or less, of truth in this.
Yet from the hour of his consecration there
began to be but one mind as to the supreme wisdom of the choice, and before untimely death cut
him down this union of sentiment had grown to
unanimity almost, if not altogether, complete.
The people's judgment, obedient to their inspired
heart, was right.

It cannot be too clearly understood that one

main cause of the unprecedented enthusiasm for Bishop Brooks was his breadth of Christian comprehensiveness. All his other splendid qualities would not have sufficed so to endear him to the public without this one. The universal heart went forth to him because he consistently and constantly declared that Christ is the head of the universal church, and that every organized body of worshipping believers, by whatever name called, has an equal right with any other to claim to be a part of the Church. It would be a most portentous mistake to interpret yesterday's events as a token of popular trend toward the exaltation of one sect at the expense of others. They afford the strongest possible rebuke to any such idea. At the same time it is unquestionable that the special branch of the Church to which the departed prelate was attached, and to which he was always devoted with special affection and unwavering loyalty, has been brought through his influ· ence into closer touch with "all sorts and conditions of men," has won a stronger hold on the community than could have been secured through any other human agency. Herein is a lesson that "churchmen" cannot heed too diligently. It is not by narrowness, but by breadth, not by ex-

clusive pretensions, but by the largest fellowship,
that the representatives of any denomination
can best promote its growth and extend its
power.

There is reason for rejoicing that Phillips
Brooks was so entirely a preacher of the gospel.
Otherwise there might be a chance to misunder-
stand yesterday's marvellous homage. Rarely,
in our generation, has a famous clergyman so
completely illustrated the apostolic words, "This
one thing I do." Some distinguished preachers
have been prominent in political discussions,
others in literature, some in temperance or educa-
tional reform : still others have won fame as sci-
entists or platform lecturers. We are not find-
ing fault with them. Oftentimes their usefulness
in extra-religious lines has been such as to fully
justify their multiform activity. But no one will
dare to say, it seems to us, that the prince of
preachers who rests in the new-made grave at
Mount Auburn could have done the world more
good if he had done anything else than minister,
in divine things to the souls of his fellow-men.
And now there is no opportunity to minimize the
significance of the demonstration that has been
made of the people's love for him. It was the

preacher of the gospel whom they honored. It was the living link between the invisible and the visible world for whom they sorrowed because they should see his face no more. Here in Boston, in this seat of science and philosophy, this alleged home of agnosticism, this mart of trade, this city that abounds in temples erected to Mammon, at whose altars high-priests of finance are said to offer sacrifices to a golden calf, here it has been proved that the man whom the citizens of the city most delight to honor is he who taught them that none of these things are worthy to be compared with the things that are spiritually discerned.

Once more, let no mistake be made in the interpretation of these great events. If worldliness needs the caution, so does religiousness no less. Bishop Brooks could never have been what he was, or been followed and trusted and loved as he was and is and is to be, but for his wonderful wisdom in bridging the gulf that too often separates the churches from the masses ; and by the word "masses" we mean to designate rich people as well as poor, learned as well as illiterate, the Back Bay and the North End, "Harvard College and the slums." He taught us all how to discrim-

inate between the letter which killeth and the
spirit that maketh alive. He showed us the essential essence of Christianity in distinction from
the man-made creeds that cluster around and
sometimes half conceal it.

About a dozen years ago Phillips Brooks delivered in Philadelphia, afterward repeating them
at Yale College and perhaps elsewhere, a series
of lectures, soon rendered accessible in book-
form, on the "Influence of Jesus." Of all his
published volumes this has probably done most to
make the English-speaking world acquainted with
his conception of religious truth. In the opening
lecture he stated that conception to be "the
fatherhood of God and the childhood of every
man to him." The preacher remarked that it was
no part of his design to prove the correctness of
this conception, for he could not understand how it
was possible for any one to study the Gospels and
remain in doubt that to reveal this truth was the
purpose of Jesus Christ in coming into the world.
"Yet," said Dr. Brooks, "if any man were in
doubt, I should only ask him to open the New
Testament with me at four most solemn places."
Then he cited the story beginning, "A certain
man had two sons"; the prayer in which the dis-

ciples were taught to say, "Our Father which
art in heaven"; the post-resurrection promise,
"I ascend unto my Father and your Father";
and the declaration made long afterward, "by
that disciple who knew him best and loved
him most," "As many as received him, to
them gave he power to become the sons
of God." The fatherhood of God and the
childhood of every man to him, that is what
Phillips Brooks conceived the truth to be which
men need to learn. When the Church is ready
to teach that, the world is ready to be taught.
And the lesson will evermore seem easier to understand by reason of the noble, tender, faithful,
unselfish, incomparable life that has been lived
among us and that abides with us still, though
the majestic form in which it was tabernacled has
gone from the city of the living to the city of the
dead.

THE BISHOP OF BOSTON.

[Jan. 31, 1893.]

Among all the tributes paid in public speech
in memory of Phillips Brooks within these past
eight days of sorrow, spontaneous, splendid, and
numberless as have been those tributes, none can
have exceeded in significance those uttered yesterday afternoon at the meeting of clergymen of
all denominations held in the historic Old South
Church on Washington Street. Everything about
that meeting was notable. The edifice was filled
to overflowing. The audience was wrought up
to the highest pitch of reverent, tender, tearful,
loving enthusiasm. The various addresses were
such as the occasion demanded. There was eloquence in the spoken words, greater eloquence
in the silent spectacle that presented itself before
any voice was lifted up. Two thoughts were in
all hearts, two themes on every speaking tongue.
The first was that the great preacher had been
the shepherd and bishop of every soul in Boston.

The second was that his death made visible what his life was spent in rendering possible,— the essential unity, despite all diversity, of the Church of Christ which is in Boston.

PHILLIPS BROOKS AT HARVARD.

[Friday, Feb. 17, 1893.]

The proposal to erect at Harvard University a memorial building in honor of Phillips Brooks is one which the friends of Harvard and of the great preacher-bishop — and who does not come under one designation or the other or both? — ought to adopt with such generous enthusiasm as will insure its speedy success. No one of the many plans suggested for commemorating this wonderful man, for expressing the gratitude universally felt toward him, and for perpetuating his visible influence, is more worthy.

His relations to Harvard were as remarkable as any single feature of his career, excepting only what he was in, and did for, Trinity Church. Outside of Trinity's pulpit the rector was more constantly and closely identified with the university at Cambridge than with any other institution or line of work. If ever there was a loyal son of an Alma Mater, Phillips Brooks was such a son of Harvard. His filial devotion was nothing less than sublime. His utmost wealth of mind and heart was poured out there unstintedly almost from the day of his matriculation to the day of his death. His classmates never tire of recounting to one another, and to a public never weary of hearing, those youthful signs of coming distinction that were fulfilled a hundred-fold. In mature and later life he loved to go back there as dearly, if possible, as the faculty, the students, and on all anniversary occasions the alumni loved to have him come. The mere announcement of his expected presence was enough to awaken eager interest in every appointed occasion. Whenever he came, he brought light and heat, the sunshine of his marvellous nature. Harvard has many grand men ready at all times to do her what service they may. Some are there all the while, others return at her call from near and from far. But there was none other among her mighty ones who could do for the foremost American seat of learning what Phillips Brooks could do, and did.

His special relations to the university as an alumnus, the more intimate identification of his life with hers, may be said to have dated from the time, not a great many years ago, when those far-reaching changes were taking place at Har-

vard which mark the most modern period,—
changes in plans of study looking to a development of the elective system previously unknown
on this continent, changes in the conception of
right relations between students and their teachers, changes in respect to the place of religious
worship in academic life; all these vast changes
being accompanied by enormous growth in en-
dowments, in number and range of professor-
ships, in number of students and the development
of such various departments as are necessary to
constitute a true university. This transition period was one of great hope, but hope mingled
with anxiety, perhaps with peril. It was at the
beginning of this crucial time that Phillips Brooks
began to impress upon Harvard University in an
especial and extraordinary degree the stamp of
his own peerless being. He was every way the
man for the place and the epoch. He had
the scholarship, the enthusiasm, the magnetism,
the breadth, the genius, the energy, the power
over young men, the intellectual and spiritual
grasp that were needed. What Harvard is
to-day is owing in immeasurable measure to
what Phillips Brooks was to Harvard in those
formative years.

APPENDIX.

[Condensed from a news article in the Boston *Daily Advertiser* of Jan. 7, 1892. Note to this book, page 82.]

In her report this year Miss Sullivan, Helen Keller's teacher, says that three years ago the little girl asked the questions, " Where did I come from ? " and " Where shall I go when I die ? " Without direct leading, her mind naturally sought for the cause of things. The explanations which this little deaf, dumb and blind girl was then able to understand did not satisfy : they only silenced her for the time being.

At last she demanded a name for the power the existence of which she had conceived in her mind. Her study of natural science had aroused her curiosity as to the origin of things, and she began to realize the vastness of Nature.

Although she had often met with the words " God," " heaven " and " soul " in the Greek stories which she dearly loved, she never asked the meaning of such words or made any comment when they occurred. Until February, 1889, no one had spoken to her of God. Then a dear relative and earnest Christian tried to tell her about God ; but, as she was unable to clothe her ideas in words which the child could comprehend, they were received as ridiculous by Helen. A few earnest words from Miss Sullivan showed Helen that she had been told something that she was not yet able to understand, and that it would be better for her not to talk about such things until she was wiser.

She had met with the expression "Mother Nature" in her reading, and for a long time after this she ascribed to her whatever she considered superhuman. She would say, "Mother Nature sends the sunshine and the rain to make the trees and the grass and the flowers grow." One day she said: "I am thinking how very busy dear Mother Nature is in the springtime, because she has so many children to take care of. She is the mother of everything,— the flowers and trees and winds. She sends the sunshine and rain to make the flowers grow. I think the sunshine is Nature's warm smile, and the raindrops are her tears."

In May, 1890, she wrote on her tablet the following: —

"I wish to write about many things I do not understand. Who made the earth and the seas, and everything? What makes the sun hot? Where was I before I came to mother? I know that plants grow from seeds which are in the ground, but I am sure people do not grow that way. I never saw a child-plant. Little birds and chickens come out of eggs. I have seen them. What was the egg before it was an egg? Why does not the earth fall, it is so very large and heavy? Tell me something that Father Nature does. May I read the book called the Bible? Please tell your little pupil many things when you have much time."

Miss Sullivan has always assumed that Helen could understand whatever it was desirable for her to know. She therefore thought it time to teach her the religious beliefs held by those with whom she was constantly coming in contact. To many questions Miss Sullivan would have to answer that there are infinitely many things that the wisest people cannot explain.

No creed or dogma has been taught Helen Keller, but Miss Sullivan has sought aid from Bishop Brooks. In a letter to Dr. Brooks Helen says : —

" Why does the great Father in heaven think it is best for us to have very great sorrow and pain sometimes ? I am always happy, and so was little Lord Fauntleroy; but dear little Jakey's life was full of sadness. And God did not put the light in his eyes, and he was blind; and his father was not gentle and loving. Do you think Jakey loved his Father in heaven more because his other father was unkind to him? How did God tell people that his home was in heaven ? When people do very wrong and hurt animals and treat children unkindly, God is grieved. What will he do to them to teach them to be pitiful and loving? Please tell me something that you know about God. I like so much to hear about my loving Father who is so good and wise."

Dr. Brooks sent the following reply : —

"I want to tell you how glad I am that you are so happy and enjoy your home so very much. I can almost think I see you with your father and mother and little sister, with all the brightness of the beautiful country about

you; and it makes me very glad to know how glad
you are.

"I am glad also to know, from the questions you ask
me, what you are thinking about. I do not see how we
can help thinking about God, when he is so good to us all
the time. Let me tell you how it seems to me that we
come to know about the heavenly Father. It is from the
power of love which is in our own hearts. Love is at the
soul of everything. Whatever has not the power of loving
must have a very dreary life, indeed. We like to think
that the sunshine and the winds and the trees are able to
love in some way of their own, for it would make us know
that they were happy if we knew that they could love; and
so God, who is the greatest and happiest of all beings, is
the most loving, too. All the love that is in our hearts
comes from him, as all the light which is in the flower
comes from the sun; and the more we love, the more near
we are to God and his love. . . .

"I told you that I was very happy because of your happiness. Indeed, I am. So are your father and your mother
and your teacher and all your friends. But do you not
think that God is also happy because you are happy? I
am sure he is. And he is happier than any of us, because
he is greater than any of us, and also because he not
merely sees your happiness as we do, but because he made
it. He gives it to you as the sun gives light and color to
the rose; and we are always most glad of what we not
merely see our friends enjoy, but of what we give them to
enjoy. Are we not?

"But God does not only want us to be happy: he wants
us to be good. He wants that most of all. He knows

that we can be really happy only when we are good. A great deal of the trouble that is in the world is medicine which is very bad to take, but which it is good to take, because it makes us better. We see how good people may be in great trouble, when we think of Jesus, who was the greatest sufferer that ever lived, and yet was the best being, and so, I am sure, the happiest being that the world has ever seen.

"I love to tell you about God; but he will tell you himself by the love which he will put into your heart if you ask him. And Jesus, who is his Son, but is nearer to him than all of us, his other children, came into the world on purpose to tell us all about our Father's love. If you read his words, you will see how full his heart is of the love of God. 'We know that he loves us,' Jesus says. And so he loved men himself; and, though they were very cruel to him, and at last killed him, he was willing to die for them, because he loved them so. And, Helen, he loves men still ; and he loves us, and he tells us that we may love him.

"And so love is everything; and, if anybody asks you, or if you ask yourself, what God is, answer, 'God is love.' That is the beautiful answer which the Bible gives.

"All this is what you are to think of, and to understand more and more, as you grow older. Think of it now, and let it make every blessing brighter because your dear Father sends it to you."

Later Helen wrote : —

"It fills my heart with joy to know that God loves me so much that he wishes me to live always, and that he gives me everything that makes me happy,— loving friends, a precious little sister, sweet flowers, and, best of all, a heart that can love and sympathize and a mind that can think and enjoy. I am thankful to my heavenly Father for giving me all these precious things. But I have many questions to ask you,—some things that I cannot understand, because I am quite ignorant; but, when I am older, I shall not be so much puzzled.

"What is a spirit? Did Jesus go to school when he was a child? Teacher cannot find anything about it in the Bible. How does God deliver people from evil? Why do the people say that the Jews were very wicked when they did not know any better? Where is heaven? My teacher says it does not matter where it is, so long as we know that it is a beautiful place, and that we shall see God there, and be happy always. But I should like to know where it is, and what it is like. What is conscience? Once I wished very much to read my new book about Heidi, when teacher told me to study. Something whispered to me that it would be wrong to disobey dear teacher. Was it conscience that whispered to me it would be wrong to disobey?"

Dr. Brooks replied : —

"I think it is God's care for us all that makes us care for one another. It is because we are in the Father's house that we know that all people are our brothers and sisters. God is very anxious that we should know that he is our Father. We can imagine something of how any father must feel whose children do not know that he is their father. He must be very anxious to tell them, and so God tries in every way to tell us. I think he writes it even upon the beautiful walls of the great house of Nature which we live in that he is our Father, as a child who found herself living in a lovely house might guess that he who built that house and put her there loved her very dearly.

"And then, again, God tells us in our hearts that he is our Father. That is what we call conscience,—God's voice in our hearts. You say that you try to do what is right in order to please your teacher, and you ask whether that is conscience. But what is it that makes you want to please your teacher? Why do you want to show her that you love her? Why do you love her? It is God in your heart that makes you grateful and makes you want to make other people happy. Your heart takes God into it, as the flower takes in the sunshine; and then, when you think God's thoughts and do God's actions, it is a sign to you that God is in you, and that you belong to him."

www.ingramcontent.com/pod-product-compliance
Lightning Source LLC
Chambersburg PA
CBHW030624270326
41927CB00007B/1290